## Independent Schools
## Examinations Board

# MIXED MATHS EXERCISES

# Year 8 (upper)

# Andrew Jeffrey

© Independent Schools Examinations Board
Jordan House, Christchurch Road, New Milton BH25 6QJ

ISBN 0 903627 07 8

Printed in Great Britain
by Stephen Austin and Sons Limited, Hertford

# INTRODUCTION

I hope that pupils will enjoy and benefit from using these mathematics exercises.

A careful glance through the exercises will reveal that new topics are constantly being introduced, and in a gradual manner wherever possible. Nevertheless, it is always a good idea for teachers to look ahead in order to pre-empt any difficulties.

***Calculators may be used in any question except where restrictions are stated in bold italics at the beginning of an exercise.***

Andrew Jeffrey

*In this exercise calculators may be used only in the brainbox question.*

1.  Calculate 32.6 × 45

2.  Calculate 15% of £45

3.  Solve the simultaneous equations

$$a + b = 7$$
$$2a - b = 5$$

4.  I roll a die twice and add the two scores.
    What is the probability that the total is 11?

5.  If $x = 5$, $y = {}^-2$ and $z = 0.5$, calculate

$$xyz + x + y + z$$

6.  Solve the equation $4t + 7 = 3 - 2t$

7.  Solve the inequality $3(w + 2) < 4 - 2w$

8.  Using any accurate method, construct a regular hexagon with sides of 5 cm.
    Briefly explain the method you use.

9.  Name **two** situations where angles have a sum of 180°

**BRAINBOX QUESTION**
Three teenagers and their maths teacher multiplied their ages together (well, there wasn't much on telly that night) and got the result 162435
What were the ages of the four people?

*In this exercise calculators may be used only in question 6(ii).*

1.  A ladder leans against a vertical wall, with the top of the ladder exactly 12 m above the ground.

    The bottom of the ladder rests on horizontal ground, 5 m from the base of the wall.

    How long is the ladder?

2.  The price of my house rises from £ 80 000 to £ 86 000

    What is the percentage increase in its value?

3.  Three identical skirts and two identical T-shirts cost £54

    Five skirts and 3 T-shirts cost £88.50

    Find the cost of each item.

4.  I roll an ordinary die twice and add the two scores.

    What is the probability that the total is

    (i) an odd number                    (ii) a prime number?

5.  If $x = 5$, $y = {}^-2$ and $z = 0.5$, evaluate $x(y - z)$.

6.  Solve the equations

    (i) $4(t + 3) = 3(t + 4) - 2(t + 6)$         (ii) $x^2 + 3 = 10$

7.  Solve the inequality $3(w + 4) < 7 - 2w$

8.  Calculate the interior and exterior angles of a regular nonagon.

9.  Point $A$ is 8 cm from point $B$ on a bearing of 075 degrees.

    Point $C$ is 6 cm from both $A$ and $B$.

    Find the two possible positions of $C$ by accurate scale drawing.

---

**BRAINBOX QUESTION**

Exactly $t$ years ago, I was $n$ years old. How old will I be in $2t$ years' time?
*(The answer is an algebraic expression rather than a number!)*

*In this exercise calculators may be used only in question 6(ii).*

1. A man needs to reach his roof by leaning a ladder against a side wall.

    The ladder is exactly 15 m long, and he needs it to reach exactly 12 m up the wall.

    How far from the base of the wall should he place the foot of the ladder?

2. (i) Copy and complete this table.

| $x$ | $x^2$ | $3x$ | $x^2 + 3x$ |
|---|---|---|---|
|  |  |  |  |
|  |  |  |  |
|  |  |  |  |

    (ii) Use the table to solve the equation $x^2 + 3x = 24$, accurate to 1 decimal place.

    (*You may add extra rows if you need to.*)

3. 3 beers and 4 cokes cost £9.30

    2 beers and 2 cokes cost £5.60

    Find the cost of each drink separately.

4. List these events in order of **increasing** probability.

    A    My birthday will be on a Friday this year.
    B    I throw a die and score a 3
    C    The first number drawn in the next National Lottery is odd.
    D    I toss an unbiased coin and get 'tails'.

5. If $x = 3$, $y = {}^-2$ and $z = 0.5$, calculate

    (i) $x(y - z)$                        (ii) $y(z - x)$

6. Solve the equations

    (i) $5(t + 3) = 3(t + 4) - 3(t + 6)$     (ii) $x^2 - 3 = 10$

7. **Accurately** construct an equilateral triangle with sides of 5 cm.

    Label the corners *A*, *B* and *C*.

    If *D* is the midpoint of *AB*, draw and measure the length of the line *CD*.

    (*This line is known as the perpendicular bisector of AB.*)

8. A cube has sides of length *x* cm.

    Find formulae for the volume *V* and the total surface area *A* of the cube.

---

**BRAINBOX QUESTION**
Could you hold your breath for a millionth of a year? Explain, showing your working.

1.   Calculate the length of the diagonal of a square of side 6 cm.

2.   (i) Copy this table.

| $x$ | $x^2$ | $4x$ | $x^2 + 4x$ |
|-----|-------|------|------------|
|     |       |      |            |
|     |       |      |            |
|     |       |      |            |
|     |       |      |            |

(ii) Choose suitable values of $x$ to help you to solve the equation $x^2 + 4x - 50 = 0$ to 3 significant figures.

3.   Bristol is on a bearing of 293° from Brighton.

What is the bearing of Brighton from Bristol?

4.   I have six players.

In how many different ways could I make up two 3-a-side teams?

5.   (i) Solve the inequalities      (a)  $3x - 4 < 7$      (b)  $3x + 6 > 0$

(ii) List the integers which satisfy both inequalities.

6.   Solve the equations

(i)  $\dfrac{5 + x}{6} = 2x$               (ii)  $\dfrac{3 - q}{q} = 4$

7.   Find the interior and exterior angles of a regular pentagon.

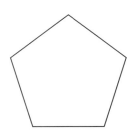

**BRAINBOX QUESTION**

An apple, a banana and a carrot cost 47p
An apple, 3 bananas and 2 carrots cost £1.02
A banana and 2 carrots cost 51p
What is the price of each item?

1.   (i) Copy this table.

| $x$ | $x^2$ | $x^3$ | $x^2 + x^3$ |
|---|---|---|---|
|  |  |  |  |
|  |  |  |  |
|  |  |  |  |
|  |  |  |  |

(ii) Choose suitable values of $x$ to solve the equation $x^2 + x^3 = 24$ to two decimal places.

(*Add extra rows if you wish.*)

(iii) Why does the equation $x^2(x + 1) = 24$ have the same solution?

2.   Solve by substitution

$$x = 3y + 2$$
$$3x + 5y = 34$$

3.   Solve the equations

(i) $5(p - 3) = 3(p + 4) - 3(p + 2)$      (ii) $^-6 = 10 - q^2$

4.   Construct **accurately** a regular hexagon in the following manner.

Draw a circle of radius 5 cm.

From the centre, draw six radii, each exactly 60 degrees apart. (*You should now have what appears to be a wheel with six spokes.*)

Now join up the six points where the radii touch the circumference of the circle to give you a hexagon.

Label the points $A$, $B$, $C$, $D$, $E$ and $F$.

5.   Measure the length of one side of the hexagon drawn in question 4.

Find and mark the point $G$, the midpoint of the line $EF$.

Now use Pythagoras' theorem to calculate the distance from $G$ to the centre of the circle.

6.   Using a method similar to that described in question 4, construct **accurately** a regular octagon.

**BRAINBOX QUESTION**

Find **two** numbers whose sum is seven less than their product?

1. List all the square numbers smaller than 200

2. Factorise

    (i) $3p^2 + 15\,pq$

    (ii) $8t + 12t^3$

    (iii) $d^2 + 7d + 10$

3. Birmingham is on a bearing of 325° from London.

    What is the bearing of London from Birmingham?

4. The equation $x^2 + 7x = {}^-10$ has a solution between ${}^-4$ and ${}^-10$

    Find this solution by trial and improvement.

5. Which is nearer to $\frac{1}{7}$, $\frac{1}{6}$ or $\frac{1}{8}$?

    Explain your answer carefully.

6. Using compasses, construct a triangle with sides of 6 cm, 7 cm and 8 cm.

    Then measure and write in the three angles.

7. The area of a semicircle is 100 cm².

    What is its diameter?

---

**BRAINBOX QUESTION**

What is the probability that **none** of my six numbers comes up in next week's National Lottery?

*(Hint: work out the probability that the first ball isn't mine, then the second, etc.)*

1. If you were to look closely at a piece of standard graph paper, you would observe that each large square measures 2 cm by 2 cm, and is actually a ten by ten grid of smaller squares.

   What is the area of each **small** square?

2. At which approximate co-ordinates do the lines $y = x^2$ and $y = 5 - x$ intersect?

3. What is 20% of 30% of 40% of £1000?

4. Solve the equation

$$3(4 - q) - 2(q + 6) = 7(4 + 2q)$$

5. The volume of water in a square-topped swimming pool is 350 cubic metres.

   If the depth of the water is 1·4 m, what is the area of the surface of the pool?

6. What is the difference between the **product** of $\frac{2}{3}$ and $\frac{1}{4}$, and the **sum** of $\frac{2}{3}$ and $\frac{1}{4}$?

**BRAINBOX QUESTION**
Estimate the number of small squares on an A4 piece of graph paper.

1.  Four computers cost £2100, £1500, £1100 and £900 respectively.

    I am offered a discount of 40% on the first machine, 30% on the second machine, 20% on the third machine and 10% on the fourth machine.

    How much change will I receive from £5000 if I buy all four computers?

2.  The top of a cereal box is 6 cm by 13 cm, and the box is $x$ cm tall.

    (i) Sketch the net of the box.

    (ii) Write down and simplify expressions for

        (a)  the volume

        (b)  the surface area of the box.

    (iii) The box has a surface area of 1182 cm$^2$

        How tall is the box?

3.  The value of my shares goes up by 10% on Monday morning, and down by 10% on Monday afternoon.

    Are they then worth more or less than at the start of the day? Explain carefully.

4.  Solve the equation

    $$y^2 + 3(6 - y) - 2(y - 4) = y(2 + y)$$

5.  Find the area of a triangle whose sides are all of length 1 cm.

    *(Hint: a diagram is probably essential to success here.)*

6.  Find out how to multiply $(a + b + c)$ by $(d + e + f)$.

---

**BRAINBOX QUESTION**
Find the sum of the integers from 1 to 50 inclusive.
*(Invent a short cut to help you.)*

1.    (i) Solve the inequalities

      (a)  $\frac{x}{2} - \frac{2}{3} < 7$

      (b)  $5 - \frac{3x}{2} < 19$

    (ii) List the integers which satisfy both of the above inequalities.

2.    A triangular prism has an isosceles right-angled triangle for its cross section, with the two equal sides 3 cm long.

    The length of the prism is 5 cm.

    Draw the net, and calculate the volume of the prism.

3.    Solve the equation

$$p^2 + 3(6 - 2p) - 2(p - 6) = p(7 + p)$$

4.    Use your calculator to work out

    (i)  $\frac{1}{2}(2.3 - 3.5)^2 - (1.4 \times 3.5)$

    (ii) $3 + 5 \div 6 - 2 \times 4$

    *(Try to find the quickest methods i.e. fewest key-presses.)*

5.    Farmer Jemmett wishes to put up a fence around a square field of area 64 m².

    He also wishes to erect a fence running diagonally across the field from corner to corner to separate the sheep from the goats.

    Find the length of fencing he needs to buy.

6.    Write the first 6 rows of Pascal's Triangle.

7.    Multiply out $(x + 1)^2$

**BRAINBOX QUESTION**
The number 100 and the number 20 are in the ratio 5:1
By adding the same number to both, I make the ratio 3:1
Which number do I add?

*Where answers are not exact, give them to 1 decimal place.*

1.    Solve the equation $x^2 + x = 7$ by trial and improvement.

2.    Find the area of a semicircle with radius 5 m.

3.    Find the next two numbers, and the $n^{th}$ term in this sequence.

$$1 \quad 4 \quad 9 \quad 16 \quad ...$$

4.    Simplify $3(x + 2) - 4(x + 1)$

5.    Solve the simultaneous equations

$$3x - 8y = 2$$
$$2x + 4y = 6$$

6.    Solve the inequality $\frac{1}{2}x - 1 > 4$

7.    Factorise fully $6x^2 + 12x$

8.    A fair coin is tossed, and a fair 4-sided spinner numbered 1, 2, 3 and 4 is spun at the same time.

List all possible outcomes.

What is the probability that a head and an even number occur?

9.    Find the length of the third side of this triangle.

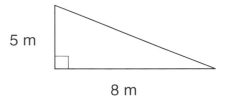

5 m

8 m

10.   I travel 10 km to work.

It takes me $p$ minutes.

   (i) Find how many hours the journey takes.

   (ii) Then write an expression for my average speed in km/h, and show that it simplifies to 600/$p$.

   (iii) The journey home takes 6 minutes longer.

Find an expression for my average speed for the whole journey.

**BRAINBOX QUESTION**
Find the sum of all the integers from 101 to 150
*(Hint: find out about a mathematician named Gauss.)*

*Where answers are not exact, give them to 1 decimal place.*

1. Solve the equation $x^2 + 3x = 20$ by trial and improvement.

2. Radius of inner circle = 3 cm; radius of outer circle = 9 cm.

   Find the shaded area.

3. Find the next two numbers, and the $n^{th}$ term in this sequence.

   **2     5     10     17     ...**

4. Simplify $4(t^2 - 1) + 3t(t - 2)$

5. Solve the simultaneous equations

$$3p + 2q = 14$$
$$4p - 2q = 7$$

6. Solve the inequality $5 - 3x < 8$

7. Factorise fully $5t^2p + 10p^2t + 20pt$

8. Find the length of the base in this triangle.

   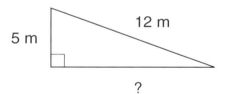

   5 m   12 m   ?

9. In a biathlon race, competitors must swim for a certain distance, and then run a further distance.

   The annual Rottingdean Biathlon involves a 2 km swim, which Norbert completes in $t$ minutes. He takes $1\frac{1}{2}$ hours to do the 5 km run.

   (i) Write down **in hours** how long the swim takes him.

   (ii) Write down and simplify an expression for Norbert's average swimming speed.

   (iii) After the race, Norbert calculates that his average speed for the whole biathlon is 2 km/h.

   Taking into account Norbert's total distance and time for the race, show that this leads to the equation

$$7 = 2\,(\,t/60 + 1.5\,)$$

   (iv) Solve the equation in part (iii).

---

**BRAINBOX QUESTION**

A bag contains 3 red, 2 blue and 2 green sweets. I remove a sweet, note its colour, do not replace it, and remove another. What is the probability that both sweets are red?

*Where answers are not exact, give them to 1 decimal place.*

1.  Solve the equation $x(x - 5) = 20$ by trial and improvement.

2.  Find the area of this sector of a circle.

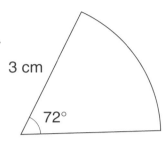

    3 cm

    72°

3.  Find the next two numbers, and the $n$th term in this sequence.

    **0.5     2     4.5     8     ...**

4.  Simplify $\dfrac{25x^2y^3}{15xy}$

5.  Solve the simultaneous equations

    $$4m - 3n = 10$$
    $$2m + 3n = {}^-4$$

6.  Solve the inequality

    $$6 + 2x < 7 - 3x$$

7.  Factorise fully

    $$a^2b^2c^2 + ab^2c + cba$$

8.  I always have tea or coffee or orange juice for breakfast.

    The probability of having tea is 0.3 and the probability of having coffee is $\frac{1}{2}$

    What is the probability of having orange juice?

9.  What is the distance between the points $({}^-4, 7)$ and $(2, {}^-1)$?

10. A tin of paint has a radius of 6 cm, and a height of 16 cm.

    How much paint can be put in the tin, to the nearest
    cubic centimetre?

    LUDUX

**BRAINBOX QUESTION**
Calculate the sum of the interior angles of a pentagon.

*Where answers are not exact, give them to 1 decimal place.*

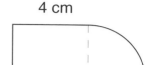

1.  Solve the equation $x^2 - 3x = 100$ by trial and improvement.

2.  Find the area of this shape, made from a semicircle
    and a rectangle.

3.  Find the next two numbers, and the $n$th term in this sequence.

    **2      6      12      20      30      ...**

4.  Simplify   $\dfrac{25y^3}{15xy}$

5.  Solve the equation $2(3x - 4) = 8$

6.  (i) Solve the inequalities $3x - 4 > 8$ and $27 - 2x > 10$

    (ii) List all the integers which satisfy both inequalities.

7.  Factorise fully $6a^2b^2 + 15ab^2c + 12abc$

8.  Find the surface area of this cuboid.

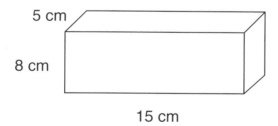

9.  What is the distance between the points ($^-3$, $^-3$) and $(2, 9)$?

10. (i) Two doughnuts and three coffees cost £1.51 altogether. Express this
        information as an equation.

    (ii) Four doughnuts and ten coffees cost £4.02 altogether. Express this information
        as an equation.

    (iii) Solve these simultaneous equations, and hence find the price of 3 doughnuts
        and 2 coffees.

**BRAINBOX QUESTION**
Calculate the sum of the interior angles of a heptagon.

*Where answers are not exact, give them to 1 decimal place.*

1.   Solve the equation $2x^2 + 3x = 100$ by trial and improvement.

2.   Find the volume of these steps.

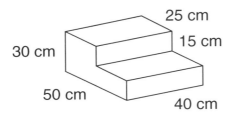

25 cm

15 cm

30 cm

50 cm

40 cm

all angles in the steps are 90 degrees

3.   Find the next two numbers, and the $n^{th}$ term in this sequence.

**3.5     4     4.5     5     ...**

4.   Simplify $\dfrac{10y^3 + 10y^3}{15xy}$

5.   Solve the equation $\frac{1}{3}(3x - 4) = 8$

6.   (i) Solve the inequalities $3x - 9 > 8$ and $57 - 4x > 8$

     (ii) List all the integers which satisfy both inequalities.

7.   Factorise fully $52a^2b^2 + 39ab^2c$

8.   Find the surface area of this cuboid.

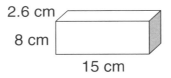

2.6 cm

8 cm

15 cm

9.   Complete the table of values for the function $y = 3x^2 - 12$

| $x$ | $^-3$ | $^-2$ | $^-1$ | 0 | 1 | 2 | 3 |
|---|---|---|---|---|---|---|---|
| $y$ | | | | | | | |

**BRAINBOX QUESTION**

The framework of a hollow cube is created from pieces of wire.
What length of wire would be needed to create a cube with volume 343 cm$^3$?

*Where answers are not exact, give them to 1 decimal place.*

1. Solve the equation $x^2 + 6 = 4$ by trial and improvement, *if you can.*

2. Find the volume of this can of cat food.

New!
MOUSE
Flavour

assume the can to be a perfect cylinder, with radius 4 cm and height 12 cm

3. Find the next two numbers and the $n^{th}$ term in this sequence.

$$3 \quad 7 \quad 11 \quad 15 \quad ... \quad ...$$

4. Simplify $\dfrac{10t^3 + 12t^3}{15xty}$

5. Solve the equation $\frac{1}{2}(3x - 6) = 16$

6. (i) Solve the inequalities $28 - 3p > 8$ and $7 < 5p + 8$

   (ii) List all the integers which satisfy both inequalities.

7. Factorise fully $34a^2b^2c + 51ab^2c$

8. Find the surface area of this cuboid.

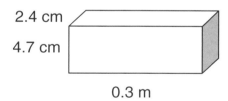

2.4 cm

4.7 cm

not to scale

0.3 m

9. Express 350 as the product of prime factors.

10. Complete the table of values for the function $y = 8 - \frac{1}{2}x^2$

| $x$ | ⁻3 | ⁻2 | ⁻1 | 0 | 1 | 2 | 3 |
|---|---|---|---|---|---|---|---|
| $y$ | | | | | | | |

**BRAINBOX QUESTION**
Calculate the sum of the interior angles of a hexagon.

1. A square has a diagonal of 8 cm.

   What is its area?

2. Find the area of this arch, correct to 1 decimal place.

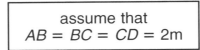

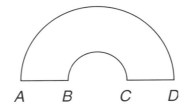

3. Find the next two numbers and the $n^{\text{th}}$ term in this sequence.

   **3    7    12    18    25    ...    ...**

4. Simplify $\dfrac{5t^3(3t)}{10xty}$

5. Solve the equation $\frac{1}{3}(6 - 3x) = 3$

6. Solve by substitution $\begin{array}{l} 3x + 2y = 18 \\ x + \ y = \ \ 8 \end{array}$

7. Factorise fully $39a^2b^2c + 26ab^2c + 13abc$

8. In a general election, the Slumber Party wins 50 000 votes.

   In a pie chart of the results they are given 20 degrees.

   > **Vote SLUMBER for a quieter life!**

   How many people voted in the election altogether?

9. Bonny and Clyde go cycling.

   Bonny is the fitter, and cycles 5 km further than Clyde, at a speed of 4 km/h, as opposed to Clyde's leisurely 1.5 km/h.

   The cyclists take exactly the same time for their journeys.

   If Clyde cycles $x$ km, then by considering the relationship between distance, speed and time, form an equation in $x$, and solve it to find the length of Clyde's cycle ride.

---

**BRAINBOX QUESTION**

Find the mean of these numbers:  0.91    $1\frac{1}{5}$    1.05    1

1.   What is the 20<sup>th</sup> prime number?

2.   Calculate, showing all working, 560 divided by 0.8

3.   If 7 thargs are worth 3.2 flumps, what are 12 thargs worth?

4.   A suit, reduced by 30%, now costs £140
     What was the original price?

5.   The ages of Bill and Hillary are in the ratio 1:3
     Monica is 5 years older than Hillary.
     If Bill is $x$ years old, and the sum of all three ages is 82, calculate each person's age.

6.   Multiply out and simplify $(4t - 3x)(3t - x)$

7.   Use Pythagoras' theorem to find, to the nearest cm, the lengths of

     (i)  $AC$

     (ii) $AG$

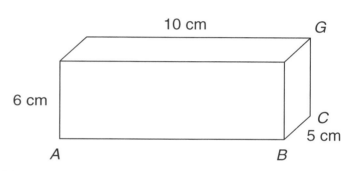

8.   Copy and complete the following tables.

     $y = 5 - 2x$

| $x$ | $^-2$ | $^-1$ | 0 | 1 | 2 |
|-----|-------|-------|---|---|---|
| $y$ |       |       |   |   |   |

     $y = \frac{1}{2}(x^2 + 5)$

| $x$ | $^-2$ | $^-1$ | 0 | 1 | 2 |
|-----|-------|-------|---|---|---|
| $y$ |       |       |   |   |   |

9.   An aircraft propeller rotates at 1500 revolutions per minute.
     A squashed fly is stuck to the propellor exactly 1.05 m from the centre.
     Find the speed of the fly in m/s (to the nearest 10 m/s).

**BRAINBOX QUESTION**
The answer is 5
What is the question? *(Try to be a bit creative!)*

*Do not use calculators for this exercise.*

1.   Find the value of 356.8 × 24

2.   Calculate $3\frac{3}{4}$ + (15% of 45)

3.   7 cans of Pepsi and 5 hotdogs cost $12.48

     2 cans of Pepsi and 10 hotdogs cost $14.28

     What is the cost of each item?

4.   Draw a circle of radius 5 cm.

     **Accurately** construct a regular nonagon inside the circle, by calculating the angle needed at the centre of the circle.

5.   Simplify $5y\,(3y - 5y)$

6.   The two shorter sides of a right-angled triangle are 7 cm and 24 cm.

     Calculate the length of the hypotenuse.

7.   (i) Calculate the volume of this cuboid.

     (ii) Calculate its surface area.

2 m

6 m

25 m

8.   A fish swims 3 km in 5 hours.

     How long would it take to swim 4 km?

**BRAINBOX QUESTION**
Sanjay is 3 times Ghita's age, but in 5 years' time he will be twice her age.
How old are they now?

1. Five people sat an examination.

   The average score was 66%.

   Fred scored only 50%. His paper was re-marked, and he then noticed that his score was exactly the same as the new form average.

   What was his new score?

2. A brick measures $x$ cm by $x$ cm by 20 cm.

   Show that the total surface area is $2x^2 + 80x$.

3. A swimming pool is in the shape of a cuboid.

   The surface measures 7 m by 25 m.

   If there are 323.75 m$^3$ of water in the pool, calculate the depth of the pool.

4. List all the integers which satisfy both of these inequalities.

   $$5(w - 3) < 9 \hspace{3cm} 3(w + 2) < 8w$$

5. If $a = 0.5$, $b = 2.88$ and $c = 500$, find $h$, where $h = \dfrac{a + b + c}{abc}$

6. Find the 100$^\text{th}$ term in this sequence.

   $$\textbf{20} \hspace{1cm} \textbf{17} \hspace{1cm} \textbf{14} \hspace{1cm} \textbf{11} \hspace{1cm} \textbf{8} \hspace{1cm} \textbf{...}$$

7. The equation $x^3 - 4x - 12 = 0$ has a solution between 1 and 3

   Find the solution by trial and improvement, giving an answer which is correct to 2 decimal places.

8. Find the perimeter of this trapezium.

   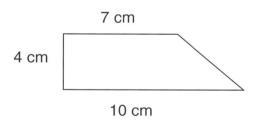

9. Copy and complete this table of values for the function $y = \dfrac{x^2}{4}$

   | $x$ | ⁻4 | ⁻3 | ⁻2 | ⁻1 | 0 | 1 | 2 | 3 | 4 |
   |---|---|---|---|---|---|---|---|---|---|
   | $y$ | | | | | | | | | |

**BRAINBOX QUESTION**
Calculate the sum of the interior angles of a decagon.

1.  In a class of 20 children, set B = {children with blue eyes}, and set G = {children who wear glasses.}

    If $n(B) = 12$, $n(G) = 4$, and $n(B'\cap'G) = 5$, draw a Venn diagram to show the relationship between the two sets.

    Find $n(B\cap G)$.

2.  Find the volume of a cylindrical swiss roll of radius 3 cm and length 15 cm.

3.  I take 30 seconds to run up a hill.

    It takes only 25 seconds to run back down the hill.

    My average speed is 1 m/s slower on the way up than on the way down.

    How many metres long is the slope?

    *(Hint: draw a table, and let the slope be x metres long.)*

4.  A cyclist travels at 12 mph for 40 minutes and then at 15 mph for 20 minutes.

    What is the average speed for the whole journey?

5.  Without using a calculator, divide twelve and one quarter by the sum of a third and a quarter.

6.  Find the $n$th term in this sequence.

    $$5 \quad 8 \quad 11 \quad 14 \quad 17 \ldots$$

7.  By finding any six points on the curve, draw the graph of $y = x^2 - 5$

8.  (a)  Factorise $2\pi rh + \pi r^2$

    (b)  Solve $x - \frac{x}{5} = \frac{16}{3}$

---

**BRAINBOX QUESTION**

Corky buys 3 blouses from Horrids, costing 23 pounds in total.
The first blouse costs a pound more than the second, which costs two pounds more than the third, which is itself in a '1/3 OFF'! sale.
How much did the third blouse cost originally?

1.  (a)  The angles in a triangle are in the ratio 7:3:2
        What is the size of each angle?

    (b)  Simplify $(2t)^3 - 2t^3$

2.  I think of a number, double it and then subtract 4
    The result is 3 times the number I first thought of. What was the number?

3.  A pair of shoes is reduced in a sale from £18 to £12.60

    (i)  What is the actual discount?

    (ii)  What is the percentage discount?

4.  Simplify
    (i)  $6(t + 7) - 3(2t - 1)$         (ii)  $5q(q + 3) - (2q - 11)$

5.  Find the 100th term in this sequence.

                 **15    12    9    6    3    ...**

6.  Calculate the area of this pizza slice.

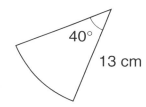

7.  By finding any six points on the curve, draw the graph of $y = \dfrac{(x + 2)^2}{3}$

8.  Solve the equations
    (i)  $\dfrac{4w}{3} + 6 = 8$         (ii)  $2^x = 64$

9.  A drawer contains 19 socks.
    Some have a red stripe, some have a blue stripe, and some have both.
    13 have a red stripe, 10 have a blue stripe, and all socks have at least one stripe.

    (i)  Draw a Venn diagram to represent this information.

    (ii)  Using your diagram, what is the probability that a sock drawn at random will have **both** a red **and** a blue stripe?

**BRAINBOX QUESTION**

Tom can row 500 metres in 1 minute 29 seconds.
How far can Tom row in an hour at the same pace?

1.  Showing your **non-calculator** method **clearly**, find the value of

    (i)  $350 \div 0.7$              (ii)  $0.625 \div \frac{5}{8}$

2.  The first 5 terms of a sequence are

    $$9 \quad 5 \quad 1 \quad ^-3 \quad ^-7 \quad ...$$

    (i)  What is the $n^{th}$ term of the sequence?

    (ii)  One term is $^-51$

    Form and solve an equation to find which term it is.

3.  A trundle wheel goes round once every metre.

    What is its radius? (to 2 decimal places)

4.  Evaluate $3\frac{1}{2} + 4\frac{3}{8} \times 2\frac{3}{5}$

5.  After a 20% increase, Anna's wage is £216 per week.

    What was her wage before?

6.  Simplify the following expressions.

    (i)  $5(q-3) - 3(2-2q)$

    (ii)  $\dfrac{3x + 2x^2 + 5x}{4x}$

    (Hint: for part (ii): can you **factorise** the numerator?)

7.  Find the mean, mode, median and range of these scores of 30 pupils.

    | score     | 1 | 2 | 3 | 4 | 5 | 6 |
    |-----------|---|---|---|---|---|---|
    | frequency | 3 | 4 | 6 | 7 | 6 | 4 |

**BRAINBOX QUESTION**
Geraldine cycles $x$ km at 12 km/h, and then walks $y$ km at 4 km/h.
Altogether she travels 44 km in 6 hours.
Find $x$ and $y$.

1.　(i)　Express four million as the product of prime factors.

　　(ii)　Hence or otherwise find the square root of four million.

2.　The length of a rectangle is 5 cm more than its width.

　　If it is $t$ cm long, and the area is 26 cm$^2$, form a quadratic equation in $t$.

　　Use trial and improvement to solve this equation correct to 3 significant figures.

3.　The diagram shows a square, side 4 cm, inside a circle.

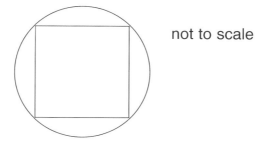

not to scale

　　Find

　　(i)　the area of the square

　　(ii)　the area of the circle

　　(iii)　the percentage of the circle which falls outside the square.

4.　The mean mass of the St. Oddbins 1$^{st}$ XI is 45 kg. Shaun '*the sheep*' Shearer, who weighs 80kg, is put off-games by matron.

　　He is replaced by a 25 gram table-football player.

　　What is the new mean mass of the team?

5.　I cycled 18 km to my friend's house.

　　She later gave me a lift home along the same route, driving at an average speed of 36 km/h.

　　The total time for both journeys was $3\frac{1}{2}$ hours.

　　What was my average cycling speed?

**BRAINBOX QUESTION**
Calculate the sum of the interior angles of a heptagon.

1. Evaluate, **without using a calculator**

   (i) $2\frac{3}{4} + 3\frac{5}{6}$        (ii) $4\frac{2}{5} - 2\frac{3}{4}$        (iii) $3\frac{1}{8} \times 1\frac{1}{5}$        (iv) $5\frac{4}{7} \div \frac{13}{14}$

2. Find the 40th term in this sequence.

   **10    16    22    28    ...**

3. What is the area of this shape, correct to 1 decimal place?

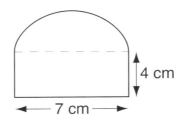

4. (i) Using 1 cm to 1 unit, draw axes numbered from 0 to 9 in the first quadrant.

   (ii) Plot the points (2,1), (3,1) and (3,3) and join them to form a triangle.

   (iii) Enlarge the triangle by scale factor 3, with centre of enlargement (0,0).

   (iv) How many times larger is the area of the new triangle than the old one?

5. Factorise fully

   (i) $5a + 10ab + 50a^2$               (ii) $3pq + 39qw$

6. Simplify

   (i) $\dfrac{25x^6}{10x^2}$            (ii) $\dfrac{3w + 6p}{9q}$

7. Solve

   (i) $\frac{1}{4}(x + 3) + \frac{1}{5}(x - 1) = 10$        (ii) $\dfrac{4f}{5} = 8 - f$

8. A bag contains 20 balls, numbered from 1 to 20

   Set P = {prime numbers} and the set T = {two digit numbers}.

   (i) Draw a Venn diagram showing where each ball goes.

   (ii) Hence or otherwise find the probability that a ball picked at random will have two digits but not be prime.

**BRAINBOX QUESTION**

What was numerically special about 9 September, 1999? When will something similar happen again?

Well done; you've reached the last exercise! Here are a few old problems to get your teeth into!

1.  I buy a second-hand car for £ n, then spend a further 60% of the cost on a major overhaul.

    The total cost is £ 9640

    Find out how much I originally paid for the car.

2.  Kim decides to run the 2 km to the local gym.

    She runs the first x km at 8 km/h, then walks the rest at 4 km/h.

    Altogether the journey takes 20 minutes.

    Form and solve an equation to find the value of x.

3.  The St. Oddbins paved courtyard is 15 m long and 14 m wide.

    In the centre there is a circular fishpond with diameter 12 m.

    Find the paved area.

4.  The hypotenuse of a right-angled triangle is 10 cm long, and the other two sides are x cm and x − 2 cm.

    Find the lengths of these two sides.

5.  *FUMES-R-US* have a lorry which is 20 metres long.

    It crosses a narrow bridge 580 metres long.

    How long will it take the lorry to cross the bridge while travelling at a constant speed of 18 km/h?

CONGRATULATIONS – YOU'VE FINISHED THE COURSE!
GOOD LUCK IN YOUR EXAMS; IF YOU'VE MANAGED TO DO ALL THESE
EXERCISES, YOU SHOULD DO VERY WELL INDEED.